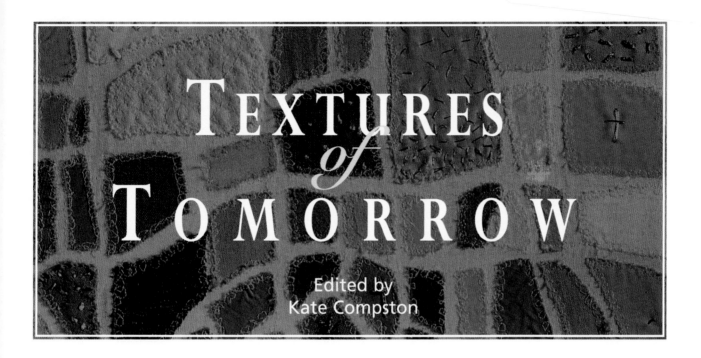

TEXTURES *of* TOMORROW

Edited by
Kate Compston

WORDS AND IMAGES ON
THE THEME OF

The United Reformed Church. 1996

INTRODUCTION

RECONCILIATION is a dynamic word: it suggests a process — a journeying ... It implies the need and the will, in all concerned parties, to change. Reconciliation is more than returning to 'how things used to be'. To be reconciled is to be made new. And to be made new is a grace, a gift.

Such an understanding has informed the creation and selection of material for this book; and the way the material is organised aims to reflect something of the dynamic (and the ever-expanding ripples) in the process of reconciliation.

In some ways, this book is the third in a series, for it features the thought-provoking embroideries of Pamela Pavitt: obviously, it is related to *Leaves from the Tree of Peace* and *Threads of Creation*.

But there are differences besides that of the organisation of material. This time, Pamela's embroidery is accompanied by the work of other artists. Craig Russell's pen and ink drawings offer a new and challenging - sometimes discomforting - perspective. Mary Tucker's calligraphy, a small reproduction of John and Christine Belderson's large triptych, and a Christmas card design by Toon van Senten, all help to enlarge our vision.

A further difference is that most of the written material is by living writers who are members - or close friends - of the United Reformed Church. Some pieces have been written in response to glimpses of Pamela's or Craig's work: occasionally, the process has worked the other way round, and the artist has been inspired by a piece of writing ... Other offerings have simply arrived! And all of us - artists, writers and editor - have been encouraged and goaded by Peter Brain and Wendy Cooper, who - working at the Church and Society office - have done a great deal of the less exciting donkey work.

May this book be a stimulant, resource and aid towards reconciliation - whoever, and wherever, you are ...

Kate Compston

Kate Compston

In a dark time the eye begins to see

3

POSITIVE CREATION

The God of all creation
embraces every cell.
The One who taught the stars to shine
feels for the dust as well.
A God of grass and sparrows,
of those abused or poor -
this God of humble majesty
attracts us to adore.

The Christ who came to show us
the way to love the light,
shows, too, how God's amazing love
dares to embrace the night.
This friend who recreates us,
and calls his friends to share,
is making one the universe
by challenges to care.

Great Spirit of creation,
exciting and alive,
enlarge our view of unity,
so that the world may thrive.
One Earth, one life, one people,
one striving after peace,
one justice and one righteousness,
one joy that shall not cease.

David Fox

MAKE YOUR CIRCLE

Make your circle around the poor, God of love;
    make your circle around the hungry, God of compassion;
    make your circle around the oppressed, God of liberation;
    make your circle around the victims of war, God of peace.

John Johansen-Berg

4

God's plan ... is to bring all creation togeth

CONSEQUENCE

CONSEQUENCE

Never mind the consequence
of what you say and do;
live your life the way you want –
the only one is you.
Community - a myth designed
to hold us in control,
denying us our freedom
by a guilt-trip on the soul;
telling us we all must care –
the strong to help the weak,
to lift them from the valley floor
and share with us the peak.

Why must morals make the pace,
and who creates the rules?
Why not look just to myself
and maximise my jewels?
'Am I my brother's keeper?'
is a question in the wind;
all accidents of birthplace:
we take what we can find.
So keep your ethics to yourself
and let me have my peace;
don't talk to me of sacrifice,
self-giving as some grace.

Turn that TV from my view;
I have no wish to see
starving wretches' dying throes
so far away from me.
And turn the TV sound down low;
the guns of war are fierce,
disturbing my serenity,
too painful for my ears.
I can't be held responsible
for silence that I keep;
don't tell me that my attitude
makes peace and justice sleep!

Stephen L Brown

AFTERWARDS

Afterwards it wasn't quite so bad
as might have been expected –
the holocaust also destroyed
every scrap of memory, produced
a sort of universal amnesia
and a human race (so far as they
remained human) with no trace
no recollection of the past,
neither history, nor any impression
of that last incredible combustion
before the impossible present where
their strange half-life continued
amidst the cold, the stench, the dust.
Only, much later, a chance discovery
of some old records - papers, microfilm –
described the green world of before the blast
somewhere called Eden, which they labelled
primitive myth of a poetic mind.

Kenneth Wadsworth

LENT DARKNESS

Dragons lurk in desert spaces
penetrating the mind with evil claw.
Serpents' teeth seek out the chinks
insidiously, relentlessly, gnawing on the bone,
searching out the interstices of muscle and sinew.

Such is the pain of the wilderness.
Alone, alone, alone,
Christ sits exhausted
in the waste place of abandoned pleas and questions
until at last
the realisation comes
that there is only
God.

In the night-time of our fears
and in our time of questioning,
be present, ever-present God.
Be present with those
camped out in the fields of hopelessness,
with refugees and homeless,
those who live lives of quiet desperation.
Be present until the desert places
blossom like the rose
and hope is born again.

Kate McIlhagga

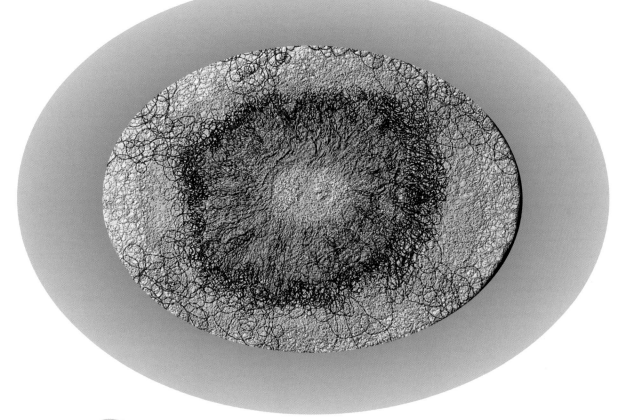

SINGING

How
can we sing a new song from
the valley of shards?
We are broken vessels
in a fissured land, indeed
we can hear
the parchment earth crack open
beneath our feet even
as we speak.

What
can we do *except*
sing songs of protest, lamentation, hope,
from split and bleeding lips
in the valley of splintered dreams?
What, except believe
that earth, like a fragile egg,
cracks open to expose
new quiverings of life?

Kate Compston

Yet alw

ARDOUR

Ardour, the soul's volcano, feels
the impulse of God's power and love.
Lava of new creation flows
and rocks the Babe sent from above.

2 Burning but unconsumed, God's word
presumed Nativity and Lent;
screened now and processed, keeps its power
to make a chaos firmament.

3 We touch it at our peril, know
we have been warned, yet in its death –
and atom-splitting power's the warmth
of the Lamb's lick that saves our breath.

4 Stretching to kiss us, though betrayed,
love links millenia to today.
The Resurrection, heaven knows
erupts from earth, rebounds our way.

Brian Louis Pearce

GOD IS WEAVING

God is crying.
The tapestry
that she wove with such joy
is mutilated, torn,
made into pieces,
its beauty worn apart with violence.

God is crying.
But see!
She is gathering the pieces
to weave something new.

She collects
the pieces from hard work;
the aim:- to defend
the initiative for peace,
the protests against injustice,
everything that seems
small and weak;
words and deeds given
as sacrifice
in hope,
in belief,
in love.

And see!
She is weaving them together
with the golden threads of joy
to a new tapestry:
a creation richer, more beautiful
than the old!

God is weaving,
patient, persistent,
with a smile
that is shimmering like a rainbow
over her face, striped with tears.
And she invites us
not only to continue
to give her
our works
with our suffering pieces –

But even more –
to sit beside her
at the loom of Jubilee
and weave
together with her
the tapestry of a New Creation.

M. Rienstra: trans. Yvonne Dahlin

'I am maki

GIFT OF TEARS

*L*ord, we give you thanks for the gift of tears:
 for tears of grief, redeeming our mourning from despair;
 for tears of anger, awakening our thirst for justice;
 for tears of laughter, celebrating our joy in living.

May the light of Christ shining through our tears
 become the rainbow of your promise,
 shedding colours of your love's bright presence
 in your grieving, struggling, laughing world.

 Peter Trow

At present we s

I was in a smooth car one evening, rolling down the motorway, with the radio on softly, crackling gently, making a little place of home by the wheel. Outside, the hot descending air, heavy at dusk, trapped the smoke of a thousand township fires; the huts and houses level as far as you could see. The smoke lingered; the smoke of wood for cooking, the smoke of tyres, paper, and who knows; the heavy, darkening air. It was the smoke of a thousand stories, of loss and sudden bad news. It was the incense of a thousand prayers that would not rise. I pressed the accelerator and hurried on, for who knows when the Spirit's wind will come and the accusing smoke rise to heaven.

Bob Warwicker

Behind the house of the Community of Sisters of the Church of Jesus Christ in Madagascar, young men were smoking drugs and drinking. They had no work, no pride in themselves, no care for anyone else. The sisters asked each man how he saw life and what talents or possibilities he felt he had. The men formed a group called the Ark - to pray, discuss and dream together. They set up two projects: shoe making and painting. Suddenly there is hope, a sense of purpose, a new self-respect and fellowship so that not only are the men happier but the whole neighbourhood feels better. And we know, as they are beginning to discover too, that all this comes from Christ, present among us, removing fear and prejudice, giving us new vision, stength, love and courage to go forward.

Eleri Edwards

ly puzzling reflections

"Do but listen .

LISTENING

LISTENING

What if we took up spades,
forks, rakes, hoes,
and went together out
of the chinkless house
of words into the
unwalled winds and wide
air, and - earth-inclined
(bowing or kneeling) -
turned with a chosen tool
the soils of quietness?

Would we have forfeited
an opportunity to grow
in understanding of the world
and of each other - make
ourselves more clear,
define and re-define
ideas, ideals - and share
the truths we think we know?

Or would we, in sifting
the earth, wondering
at its variety, its textures
(clay that enfolds and holds, lime
that breaks its cling, sand
that lets go,
mixed fertile loam) ....
would we have chanced, in time
by quiet mindfulness, upon
a deeper way of knowing?
Human amidst the humus
(yes, in our element)
would we not be at one
and thus, and thus
more rootedly
at home?

Kate Compston

Lord God,
this we have learned in the community of faith,
for this we give you thanks:
Until we hear with each other's ears
your word is indistinct, unclear.
Until we see with each other's eyes
we live in shadowed half-light.
Until we walk as pilgrim friends
we stumble and are quick to fall.
Until we love
and let love conquer all mistrust and fear
we are pale shadows of the Christ we serve.

Give us ears and eyes and strengthened steps
and make our common search for truth
a gift of love we offer to each other.

Donald Hilton

It is when you are lost for words that I hear your voice:
When you are speechless at the hurt of creation,
When you have moved from easy concern to the pain of
        compassion,
When you know you are weak,
When you can do and say nothing,
It is then that you are open to the power of the Spirit in you;
The power made perfect in the weakness of a cross.

Do not despair:
The groaning world is pregnant with possibility.
Because of your hurt there will be healing,
Because of your mourning there will be comfort.

The way of the cross leads to a garden at daybreak,
        and a familiar voice calling you by name.

I will take your groaning and make it a prayer.
I will take your silence and give you words to say.
I will take your sadness and put a song on your lips.
And for my people and for my world, my will shall be done.

Peter Trow

EPHPHATHA

WE FACE EACH OTHER

*W*e face each other
across a raw divide.
The chasm of our anger
filled with the bones
of old hatreds.

The wounded earth
spews out our greed
in acrid smoke.
The gaping world cries out in pain.

The upward surge of birds in flight,
wheeling and dancing
in the sun,
the sound of geese
strung across an empty sky,
the scent of blossom on the wind,
gifts of a generous Creator,
to lift, to call, to heal.

Kate McIlhagga

CHOSEN PEOPLE

*L*ord, you are my Lord, and my enemy's.
He looks like you, and names you in his prayer
as I do in whose gut the venom is.
You hang upon his wall, perfume his lair.

Through our contention you are torn in two,
yet in your suffering reach out to each.
Why do I let the enemy fill my view
when I could see you standing in the breach,

the antidote to our hate, reconciling
twin worlds of us, twin anger thrust with fear,
contrariness and Shimei-like reviling,

a Hillel's gentleness and the austere
God of the burning spirit, with the smiling
countenance through my enemy made clear?

Brian Louis Pearce

'Come closer to

An old Hindu saint settled under two trees in country infested by robbers. He called it Shantineketan, the Home of Peace. The robbers thought he must have buried treasure. One crept towards him, dagger drawn, as he sat in meditation. The old man opened his eyes. There was no fear in them, only love. The robber dropped his dagger and fell to his knees. The old man rose and put his arms around the would-be murderer in token that he accepted him as a disciple.

At the beginning of my second year in college, I witnessed a miracle. It happened when Ed Wills and Eberhard Eichner faced each other for the first time. Ed had been a U.S. bomber pilot; Eberhard had served with an anti-aircraft unit of the Luftwaffe. They had been allotted adjacent rooms in Cheshunt College, Cambridge; for the next three terms, they were to be under the same roof, working, worshipping, eating together. I could see what was passing through their minds when they met: 'This is an enemy'. I remember hearing Ed say to Eberhard: 'My mother was praying for me to be saved from you, while your mother was praying for you to be saved from me.' Within a few days, these former enemies had become friends. It's always reminded me of the miracle Paul saw happening between Jew and Gentile: "Christ Jesus ... made the two one, and in his own body of flesh and blood has broken down the enmity which stood like a dividing wall between them." *(Ephesians 2:14)*

Basil E. Bridge

PRAISE GOD FOR LOVE

Praise God for love!
- for love which turns us to one another
to look with surprise into the eyes of a different face
and to see one who belongs to us.

Praise God for love!
- for love which draws us together,
out of strangeness and indifference,
to find friendship and union.

Praise God for love!
- for love which touches us from God,
reaching across the divide, defying the distance,
bringing us close, uniting us to God.

Michael Durber

PALM SUNDAY

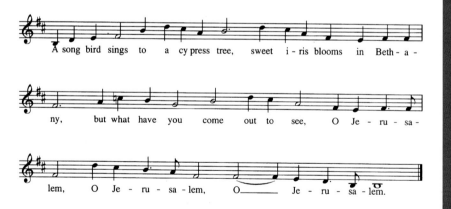

A song-bird sings to a cypress tr
sweet iris blooms in Bethany,
but what have you come out to see,
O Jerusalem?

To pilgrim shout and answering bray
he's riding down the hill today
with sorrow in his heart, to say,
O Jerusalem!

Will you destroy with cries obscene
the life of this young Nazarene
in April when the woods are green?
O Jerusalem!

A man of all men brave and true,
he'll hear the hateful things you do
and never cease from loving you,
O Jerusalem.

If you restrain the foolish crowd,
'ere love is laid beneath its shroud
the very stones will shout aloud,
O Jerusalem!

Weep not for him as he goes by,
some mother's son condemned to die;
for you and for your children cry,
O Jerusalem.

Had you but known the way that lies
to peace beneath these ancient skies!
But no, 'tis hidden from your eyes.
O Jerusalem!

Derrick Barber - words and music

"Take up your cro

REACH OUT

ACT OF REMEMBRANCE

THE GOODS

REACH OUT

Reach out your hands, Jesus,
lifted up on the cross.
On one side reach to the Israeli Jew,
longing for security and peace.
On the other side
reach to the Palestinian Arab,
longing for rights and a homeland.
On one side reach to the Christians,
your followers, disciples of your way.
On the other side, reach to the Muslims,
people of the Book, inheritors of the Covenant.
Reach out your hands in reconciling love;
reach out your hands on the cross,
sign of costly redemption.
Reach out
and draw us to yourself,
eternal love.

John Johansen-Berg

ACT OF REMEMBRANCE

In the heat of memory we recall
that for every victory
there is a loss;
that for every ceasefire,
there is a sniper;
that for every liberation,
there is a prison;
that for every peace agreement,
there is continued conflict,
if not above our skies,
if not in our waters,
if not in these islands,
if not on our doorstep,
then in some forgotten field.
We will remember them ....

Janet Lees

THE GOODS

This joker throws the blinds up, soon as blink,
seeing the dark in you, lets in his light.
There's one knows all about you, yet won't shrink.

Love knows your best and worst sides interlink.
It takes the worst and still lives with the sight.
This joker throws the blinds up, soon as blink.

His taking you on trust, it makes you think
of what you might be if your heart was right.
There's one knows all about you, yet won't shrink.

The creatures of his passion shed their kink,
quarrels their cause, devils their dynamite.
This joker throws the blinds up, soon as blink.

That you become the one you like to think
is thanks to him, who wines a thief tonight.
There's one knows all about you, yet won't shrink.

Love blossoms best where there's the greatest stink.
Deadnettle's purple blooms where there was blight.
This joker throws the blinds up, soon as blink.
There's one knows all about you, yet won't shrink.

Brian Louis Pearce

THE DEFENDERS

*W*alls are of prime importance,
the rulers stressed.
Maintenance is essential.
Every man, woman and child
must carry buckets, shovel cement, set up the broken glass,
acquire building skills and devote all leisure
to the city wall.
If your suburbs spread –
for we do not wish to limit you –
simply build another rampart further out
making sure that it too can resist sudden attack.
Gates we must have, naturally,
for there will be trade and journeys.
Let them be of iron.
Appoint guards for the gates.
They should be of keen eyesight and quick to sound the alarm
to which you will rally as a body.
Dogs, however, should be muzzled
and you yourselves tie scarves over your mouths
lest a word across the wall somewhere betray us.

We were obedient.
But when the rightful ruler took his place
he said, Take down the walls.
Open the gates. Let the children sing.
Prepare a feast and give the poor first helpings.
Invite the next village. Talk to the outer tribes.

We didn't know what to do.
Our training only equipped us for defence.
Walls are hard, we don't know how to unbuild.
And as for outer tribes,
who knows their language?

He's good, no doubt, the liberating ruler,
and indeed it was in fear we built the walls,
but we are even more afraid
to remove our scarves and smile.

Anne Ashworth

Christ has broken dow

Basel, Whitsun 1989, European Ecumenical Assembly. During a session of one of the small working groups on the theme "The abolition of the institution of war - building services for peace", one of the participants - struck by the audacity of the plan which he himself had just been helping to formulate asked: " ... What are we to do about our conflicts and antagonisms? We can't just pretend that they don't exist. What is to become of all the horrors which we have inflicted on each other in the past? All that won't just be forgotten; that is bound to surface again." "I can only tell you what I am going to do," quietly replied one of the delegates. "I will go over to the other side and offer my person as a sign and seal of the reconciliation for which I am asking. I am going to offer my service as ecumenical service for the Shalom by which we all live."

TUMBLING WALLS

*H*eaven's walls at times seem far too high –
    It's hard to see God's throne;
For fear and darkness take a hold
    And we are left alone.
And yet those walls come tumbling down
    As we in Christ believe;
Let's find fresh faith and hope and love
    And God's good grace receive.

Church walls within can soon divide
    All those who should be one;
For arrogance and pious pride
    Have all too often won.
And yet those walls come tumbling down
    As we in Christ can see:
A oneness which rejoices in
    God's rich diversity.

The walls of hatred in our world
    Destroy the ways of peace;
For humankind seems bent on war
    And strife that will not cease.
And yet those walls come tumbling down
    As we to Christ pay heed,
And give ourselves with selfless love
    To serve a world of need.

Richard Cleaves

MARY OF BETHANY

MARY OF BETHANY

COMPLEMENTARY (For ASW)

Like minds proceed, no doubt, on parallel lines,
but yours and mine are complementary:
your genius is mathematic; mine
(such as it is) is verbal, literary.
Your attitude and habit are creative,
green-fingered, musical, artistic,
and your haphazard world reveals your nature
spontaneous, untidy, optimistic.
Less sanguine, I accept convention's norms,
like things in proper order, neat and square,
even my verse prefers traditional forms,
I hitch my wagon to familiar stars.
And following our separate ways we've found
two semi-circles make a perfect round.

Kenneth Wadsworth

The girls' High School and the boys' Grammar School in Chesterfield were adjacent to each other and separated by a strong stone wall. The large stones of this wall were held together by mortar. When I started at that school, the wall was complete; and by the time that I left, the wall was breached in many places. That wall was broken down, not out of anger or frustration and not by our using brute force on it. No heavy instruments were used against it. But over the years we carefully and persistently loosened the mortar between the stones in order to pass through notes making assignations, and letters declaring our undying love. Before I left, that wall fell down all by itself. It was love that brought it down.

Kathleen M Richardson

He needed me, that gentle man. He needed me to sit, equal at his feet; to listen and reflect his thoughts in the mirror of my woman-love. It was this that made me love him so: this, not hidden under his man-strength, but open, humble, without shame, his need of me.

With him there was no avoidance of the obvious: tension of female and male, mutual delighted attraction of opposites. The others felt it too, my friends. With this man as no other, we knew ourselves as women; he, with us, himself a man, and realised God's image in us: this polarity.

Yes, it was this that day, which shocked them! Not the extravagance of the gesture, but that I, a woman, should pour out perfume over his feet, filling the room with the scent of my love for him. Was it hysteria in me? Shameless display? Even careless contempt for the poor?

The anonymous *they* will always say such things. Anointing his body for burial, he said. A truth I had not understood until he spoke it. My salute to one about to die! My passionate uncomprehending "yes" to his incarnate flesh! Just so do acts of love precede our understanding.

Alan Gaunt

We belong to one anoth

TENDERNESS

Tenderness, the ability to listen, peace making, imaginative writing, the cherishing of beauty – these are often thought of as feminine gifts ... We now have to ensure their proper place .... we may need to revise our style of church meetings, giving more time for quietness, for a sharing of the heart and not just of the argument ... We are also being challenged to re-examine our usual imagery for God as we approach the mystery. Perhaps by grace we shall find new words for a new century, words that no longer carry the masculine emphasis of tradition.

Bernard Thorogood

OFFERING

I offer you myself and mean it honestly
but you will never pierce, nor I, my mystery.

And you are dark to me; if I should draw too near
your silent forest's edge in trust, might wolves appear?

Between us I now set these words, this poetry,
this artful enterprise, which shields my honesty.

But more: if love would grasp this making from my own
mind's dark, our minds might mesh, transcending flesh and bone.

And we, though still each one one's self momentarily
might find ourselves conjoined within art's trinity.

Three forces of one power: me, the poem, you – bound
from an eternal source leaping from holy ground.

Alan Gaunt

RECONCILED

I had a dream that I shall not forget.
I spoke to someone quite unknown to me
About a friend she'd lost – for whom she mourned.

We looked together at his photograph,
And something drew us to each other then,
And so to him. Somehow I knew him, too.

Muriel Grainger

to one body

ELDER BROTHER

ELDER BROTHER

*H*ow long before the Elder Brother turned,
came to himself, and shared his father's joy,
repenting of his jealousy and pride?
How long before he too could feel at home,
saw, though unloving, he was greatly loved:
the dance and music also called for him?

Basil E Bridge

PRODIGAL

PRODIGAL

*H*oly God, I confess
   that I'm not very good at confession.
   Do I really have all of these shortcomings?
   Is a list like this relevant to our relationship?
   Holy God, I confess
   that I'm not very good at saying sorry.
   I can mumble it under my breath,
   but eyeball to eyeball is difficult.
   Holy God, I confess
   that I'm not very good at forgiveness.
   I keep lists of the failings of others,
   but I don't like to see my part in discord.
   Holy God, I confess
   that I need your holiness in me,
   that I may offer forgiveness to others
   and grasp your new opportunities for life.

Janet Lees

*G*od, like the prodigal's father,
you are not content
simply to wait for my return.
You journey to meet me,
requiring nothing
except my desire to come home.
You embrace me and kiss me,
place the costly ring of acceptance
on my finger,
and enfold me in the rich robe
of your unexpected, undeserved
and overwhelming love.
I am the guest of honour
at your celebration feast.

Peter Trow

After he had kissed and wept over his brother

faMily likeness

You bore me in pain, mother,
in sweat and squalor
in a steamy outhouse
on the straw.

You nurtured me in love, mother,
taught me to care
for my brothers and sisters –
and my heavenly Father too.

Surely you must recognise
that I have other mothers,
other sisters and brothers
whose family resemblance
is so striking
you know at once
who is their Father.

God, our mother, father, sister, brother,
help us to recognise
other members of your extended family.
May we see the likeness to Jesus in each other
and may we grow more like him every day.

Carol Dixon

REACH OUT

Reach out my hand to touch
My neighbour, friend,
Or kith and kin.

Not quite;
Not far enough;
The gap's too great.
So I must lean
Further and further,
Hand stretching out to hand.

What if I fall;
Lose balance and
        Upset
My equilibrium?

Perhaps I shall have to change my ground ...

But do I stand on holy ground?

Donald Hilton

God of our relating
thank you
for hands across the table
for hands across the sea
for hands around the world

thank you
for eyes meeting across a room
for eyes opened to different lifestyles
for eyes shining in new friendships

thank you
for ears that can hear the beating of a heart
for ears that pick up the cries of the voiceless
for ears that respond to the pulses of the world

thank you

Kate Compston

LANDMINES

Dead old tree stumps –
the legacy of war. Red young leg stumps
stumble on to peace.

Janet Lees

God has enlisted

CHANCING ONE'S ARM

CHANCING ONE'S ARM

I n 1492, two prominent Irish families, the Ormonds and Kildares, were in the midst of a bitter feud. Besieged by Gerald Fitzgerald, Earl of Kildare, Sir James Butler, Earl of Ormond, and his followers, took refuge in the chapter house of St. Patrick's Cathedral, Dublin, bolting themselves in. As the siege wore on, the Earl of Kildare concluded that the feuding was foolish. Here were two families worshipping the same God, in the same church, living in the same country, trying to kill each other. So he called out to Sir James and, as an inscription in St. Patrick's says today, 'undertooke on his honour that he should receive no villanie'.

Wary of 'some further treacherie', Ormond did not respond. So Kildare seized his spear, cut away a hole in the door and thrust his hand through. It was grasped by another hand inside the church, the door was opened and the two men embraced, thus ending the family feud.

The expression 'chancing one's arm' originated with Kildare's noble gesture. There is a lesson here for all of us who are engaged in 'family feuds', whether brother to brother, language to language, nation to nation. If one of us would dare to 'chance his arm', perhaps that would be the first crucial step to the reconciliation we all unconsciously seek.

Toon van Santen of the Netherlands, who designed the Christmas card below, writes: The bridge refers to the famous Ottoman Bridge in the town of Mostar in Bosnia, which connects two districts: Croatia is on the west side of the river and the Muslims on the east side. They lived peacefully together for a long time, but during the recent war, there was fierce fighting between them, and the beautiful bridge was blown up. That caused the severe separation which is still going on.

So this card shows the wish for reconciliation:- the Holy Family crossing the bridge to close the gap, and the Christmas angel trying to bring both groups of people together by repairing the Christmas banner. The word 'PAX' was destroyed by the rubble from the bridge, but the angel tries to restore 'PAX' in the banner, which - in a Latin version - is saying, "Glory to God in the highest and peace on earth and goodwill to all humankind". On the right side of the bridge is a mosque for the Muslims, and on the left a church symbolizing the religion of the Christians. Hence the Christmas wish – reconciliation between peoples of two religions.

PRAYER ROSARY

Hiroshima,
 Bosnia,
 Belfast,
 the names slip
 through our fingers,
 like blood-stained beads.

As we tell the story,
tell us,
tell us,
tell us
the way to peace.

Saigon,
Sarajevo,
Rwanda,
still they come,
countless numbers:
people hounded,
refugees tramping the road
out of hell, into hell.

Where will it stop?
Show us,
show us,
show us
the way to peace.

Five for sorrow,
ten for joy,
may what has been
sown in pain
be reaped in hope.

Kate McIlhagga

Have do

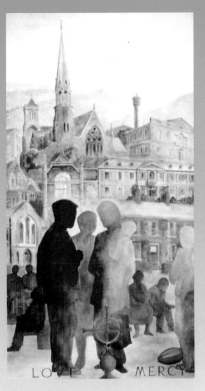

TRIPTYCH

John Belderson and his daughter, Christine, created this triptych, which measures 7 by 9 feet. It was commissioned by the Halifax United Reformed Church Group, and is housed in Park URC. It represents the life and community of Halifax in general, and the place and influence of the four churches, along with other Christian traditions, and the Muslims, in the town. Park URC has reached the end of a long project to convert its buildings for multi-purpose use - for the churches, the community, and for commerce. Surrounding Park is a large, established Moslem community of Pakistani origin, with its own fairly new mosque (see centre panel: the mosque and minaret are right of centre, and Park URC and spire are left of centre). The three central figures stand for the coming together of the local people and the Muslims. This has been, and still is, a process of reconciliation. The 'Love Mercy' (along with 'Act Wisely' and 'Do Justly') come from the motto around the Halifax Town Hall entrance portico. Nineteenth century members of Park gave much wise leadership to the town.

A MONK'S DREAM

Jim Garrison, an American theologian, once told this story: A monk had a dream. He was walking down a street when a plane flew overhead and dropped a bomb. Instinctively everyone knew it was a nuclear weapon, and all scattered - except the monk. He felt he must catch the bomb before it exploded and destroyed everyone. He caught it, and it turned to bread in his hands. He broke the bread and shared it, seeking out those who had run away and drawing them back into community.

Take our hatreds: make them into handshakes
Take our prejudices: make them into peace-offerings
Take our arguments: makes them into alliances
Take our battles: make them into bonds
Take our misunderstandings: make them into music
Take our divisions: make them into dances
Take our schisms: make them into songs.

Kate Compston.

A NEW VISION OF CREATION

Creation renewed, its emptiness filled;
Its brokenness healed, as God at first willed.
Old voices of chaos to order rescored,
With Christ as the root of each resonant chord.

Our vision is clear, but actions are dark;
We wound and destroy our precious earth-ark.
We break down our forests and poison our streams,
We murder our children and shut out our dreams.

Come, Spirit of power, and change us, we pray,
For we would be changed and walk in the day.
Come, kindle within us our love and our care;
Teach us to uphold all creation in prayer.

Then translate our prayer to action and deeds,
Commitment to care for this world and its needs.
Come, Lord, recreate us, and help us to play
Our part with you, making creation's new day.

David Fox

Creator God ...

let there be earth
    for us to respect and love
    as we seek to conserve its energy
        and resources
    for children yet to come

let there be fish and animals
    to be partners with us on the earth
    sharing our land, sea and air

let there be people
    who as your creatures
    have not lost their sense of dependence
    and who as creators
    are responsible protectors of life

David Jenkins

This gospel of reconciliation has bee

Mother of all creation, help us to see how we have betrayed you;
when for vanity we wear rich jewels whilst children starve;
when for pride we drive fast cars whilst refugees lack a home;
when for fashion we buy furs and whole species of endangered ....

Mother of all creation, pour out your Spirit upon us
that the desert may be irrigated and become a place of lush vegetation,
that there may be justice and righteousness in the wilderness
and, springing from them, trust and peace in the fruitful field.
So may your people come to the place of reconciliation
and all live secure together, the animals, the people,
in a place of pure streams and quiet fields of peace.

John Johansen-Berg

AT-oNE-MENT DANCE

The world shall dance unshackled
and all creation sing for joy.

Ears and hands will be opened wide
in the welcoming household of God.

There will be a gathering in of the creatures -
small and large, weak and strong, swift and sluggish.

All shall meet playfully,
delighting in surprises ....

Stones shall shout aloud
and trees clap their hands.

Rainbows shall uncurl, rivers take wing,
and a wren's feather trip the ravening lion.

The bat shall take soundings in the ocean depths,
and the rhinoceros swing through the cedar's branches.

With tenderness shall the ant suckle the elephant,
and human children open their petals to the sun.

The whole household shall laugh and be glad
at these experiments and reversals.

And when all are returned to their original powers,
they will each know the truth of their neighbours.

And every one will be seen by the others
as all are seen by God -

as beautiful and sacred,
having a purpose and value, precious beyond words.

And then shall the world dance unshackled
and all creation sing for joy.

Kate Compston

EARTH SONG

EARTH SONG

I am a child born of fire
for all the earth's
beginnings
sing in me.

I am a child out of time
born of pain
for all the earth's deaths
end with me.

I am a child born of love
out of light,
for you meet me here.

I am a child full of joy
born to live
and all the earth's surprises
dance in me.

I am a child born of spirit
wholeness unfolding
adorable silence
and all the earth's journeys
well up in me.

Erna Colebrook

'You must

TOO GREAT FOR ME

God, you are too great, too everywhere,
beyond the furthest nebula you touch
the dark, and all the stars you bear
like dust. For me it is too much.

God, you are too old. Behind the page
of our short history your volumes throng
with slow unfolding. Age after age
your calendar. For me it is too long.

God, you are too strong. Making the atoms spin
and every living thing run to its fate;
lifting the moons, shaking out the din
of thunder sheets. For me you are too great.

God, you are too just. You show our law
is fussy and too mean. You see the heart,
and every silent curse and hidden flaw
is plain to you. We are too far apart.

Come, Alpha, at a dated dawn,
Come, Mighty, to be flogged and torn,
Come, Justice, as the priesthood's pawn.
For us you were a little child
that great and small be reconciled.

Bernard G Thorogood

Suppose all the pieces of the true cross
around the world were suddenly to sprout,
bursting into leaf again, the world would be
green like a garden planted in Eden
and mankind unfallen find better fruit
than the sour apple of disobedience.

Kenneth Wadsworth

Because of our faith in Christ and in humankind, we must apply our efforts to the construction of a more just and humane world. And I want to declare emphatically: such a world is possible. To create this new society, we must present outstretched, friendly hands, without hatred, without rancour – even as we show great determination, never wavering in the defence of truth and justice. Because we know that seeds are not sown with clenched fists. To sow we must open our hands.

FAITH IN CHRIST

Adolpho Perez Esquivel

THE BRIGHT WIND OF HEAVEN

The bright wind is blowing, the bright wind of heaven,
 And where it is going to, no-one can say;
 But where it is passing our hearts are awaking
 To grope from the darkness and reach for the day.

The bright wind is blowing, the bright wind of heaven,
 And many old thoughts will be winnowed away;
 The husk that is blown on the chaff of our hating,
 The seed that is left is the hope for our day.

The bright wind is blowing, the bright wind of heaven,
 The love that it kindles will never betray;
 The fire that it fans is the warmth of our caring,
 So lean on the wind - it will show us the way.

Cecily Taylor

32 Make fast with bonds of peace the unity which the Spirit gives